SHORT CIRCUITS
IN
THE HOPE VALLEY

by

JOHN N. MERRILL

Maps and photographs by John N. Merrill.

TRAIL CREST PUBLICATIONS

1992

TRAIL CREST PUBLICATIONS Ltd., WINSTER, MATLOCK, DERBYSHIRE. DE4 2DQ

 Winster (0629) 650454
FAX Winster (0629) 650416

Concieved, edited, typeset, designed, paged, marketed and distributed by John N. Merrill.

© Text and routes - John N. Merrill 1992.
© Maps - John N. Merrill 1992.
© Photographs - John N. Merrill 1992.

First Published - May 1990.
This reprint - May 1992
ISBN 0 907496 61 X

Please note : The maps in this guide are purely illustrative. You are encouraged to walk with the appropriate Ordnance Survey map as detailed for each walk.

Meticulous research has been undertaken to ensure that this publication is highly accurate at the time of going to press. The publishers, however, cannot be held responsible for alterations, errors or omissions, but they would welcome notification of such for future editions.

Typeset in - Bookman - bold, italic and plain 9pt and 18pt.

Printed by - John N. Merrill at Milne House, Speedwell Mill, Miller's Green, Wirksworth, Derbyshire. DE4 4BL

Cover sketch by John Creber - "Winnats Pass"
© Trail Crest Publications Ltd. 1992.

 An all British product.

ABOUT JOHN N. MERRILL

John combines the characteristics and strength of a mountain climber with the stamina and athletic capabilities of a marathon runner. In this respect he is unique and has to his credit a whole string of remarkable long walks. He is without question the world's leading marathon walker.

Over the last twenty years he has walked more than 125,000 miles and successfully completed more than a dozen walks of a least 1,000 miles or more. His six major walks in Great Britain are -

Hebridean Journey........ 1,003 miles.
Northern Isles Journey......913 miles.
Irish Island Journey ....1,578 miles.
Parkland Journey.......2,043 miles.
Land's End to John o' Groats.....1,608 miles.

and in 1978 he became the first person to walk the entire coastline of Britain - 6,824 miles in ten months.

In Europe he has walked across Austria - 712 miles - hiked the Tour of Mont Blanc, completed High Level Routes in the Dolomites and Italian Alps, and the GR20 route across Corsica in training! Climbed the Tatra Mountains and walked in the Black Forest. He has walked across Europe - 2,806 miles in 107 days - crossing seven countries, the Swiss and French Alps and the complete Pyrennean chain - the hardest and longest mountain walk in Europe, with more than 600,000 feet of ascent!

In America he used The Appalachian Trail - 2,200 miles - as a training walk, before walking from Mexico to Canada via the Pacific Crest Trail in record time - 118 days for 2,700 miles. Recently he walked most of the Continental Divide Trail and much of New Mexico; his second home. In Canada he has walked the Rideau Trail - Kingston to Ottowa - 220 miles and The Bruce Trail - Tobermory to Niagara Falls - 460 miles.

John set off from Virginia Beach on the Atlantic coast, and walked 4,226 miles without a rest day, across the width of America to Santa Cruz and San Francisco on the Pacific coast. His walk is unquestionably his greatest achievement, being, in modern history, the longest, hardest crossing of the U.S.A. in the shortest time - under six months (178 days). The direct distance is 2,800 miles.

Between major walks John is out training in his own area - The Peak District National Park. He has walked all of our National Trails many times - The Cleveland Way thirteen times and The Pennine Way four times in a year! He has been trekking in the Himalayas five times. He created more than a dozen challenge walks which have been used to raise more than £300,000 for charity. From his own walks he has raised over £100,000. He is author of more than one hundred walking guides which he prints and publishes himself, His book sales are in excess of 2 1/2 million. He has created many long distance walks including The Limey Way, The Peakland Way, Dark Peak Challenge walk, and Rivers' Way.

CONTENTS

Page No.

INTRODUCTION

The Hope Valley was where I began to walk in the countryside and learn the thrill and excitement of discovering historical buildings, wild life and flowers, as well the joy of exercise. Every weekend I would drive or cycle from Sheffield and pass the Fox House Inn before reaching the justly famous, Surprise View. Here I would stop for a few moments, with Millstone Edge on my right, and gaze up the valley. Hathersage and the River Derwent lay ahead, before the impressive slopes of Win Hill, Lose Hill and the Peakland Ridge running up the eastern side to be crowned by Mam Tor. The western side not so high but still impressive with Offerton and Bradwell Moors. The valley floor littered with farms and the attractive villages of Hope and Castleton.

It is a walker's haven with countless walks - beside rivers, up lofty peaks, through and around historical villages, and onto remote moorland with extensive views. Selecting my favourite walks over the years, I have endeavoured, with the chosen ones, to illustrate the variety of the walking in the valley and take you to all the major places. Some are historical village walks to learn and appreciate the character of Castleton and Hathersage. Others take you up the hills from different approaches, while some take you onto moorland where the only sound above maybe a skylark or the silent whoosh of a glider.

The valley contains some of the finest walking in the Peak District - get your boots on and set off to explore one of England's richest hiking areas. Have a good walk and may the sun be always out and the wind from behind.

HAPPY WALKING!

John N. Merrill

The Peak District. 1992.

ABOUT THE WALKS

Whilst every care is taken detailing and describing the walk in this book, it should be borne in mind that the countryside changes by the seasons and the work of man. I have described the walk to the best of my ability, detailing what I have found on the walk in the way of stiles and signs. Obviously with the passage of time stiles become broken or replaced by a ladder stile or even a small gate. Signs too have a habit of being broken or pushed over. All the route follow rights of way and only on rare occasions will you have to overcome obstacles in its path, such as a barbed wire fence or electric fence. On rare occasions rights of way are rerouted and these ammendments are included in the next edition.

The seasons bring occasional problems whilst out walking which should also be borne in mind. In the height of summer paths become overgrown and you will have to fight your way through in a few places. In low lying areas the fields are often full of crops, and although the pathline goes straight across it may be more practical to walk round the field edge to get to the next stile or gate. In summer the ground is generally dry but in autumn and winter, especially because of our climate, the surface can be decidedly wet and slippery; sometimes even gluttonous mud!

These comments are part of countryside walking which help to make your walk more interesting or briefly frustrating. Standing in a farmyard up to your ankles in mud might not be funny at the time but upon reflection was one of the highlights of the walk!

The mileage for each walk is based on three calculations -

1. pedometer reading.
2. the route map measured on the map.
3. the time I took for the walk.

I believe the figure stated for each walk to be very accurate but we all walk differently and not always in a straight line! The time allowed for each walk is on the generous side and does not include pub stops etc. The figure is based on the fact that on average a person walks 2 1/2 miles an hours but less in hilly terrain.

NORTH LEES HALL

CRICKET MATCH - HATHERSAGE

CASTLETON VILLAGE
WALK - 4 MILES

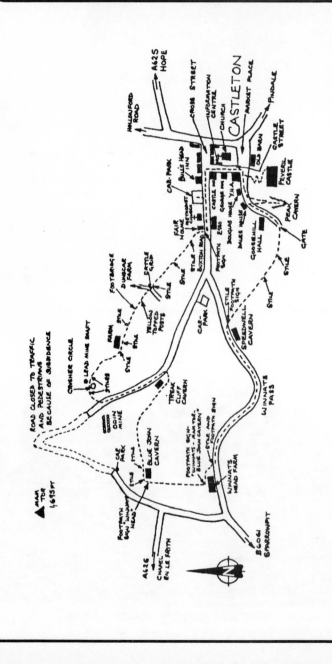

CASTLETON VILLAGE WALK
- 4 Miles - ALLOW 2 HOURS,
LONGER IF VISITING THE CAVERNS.

 1:25,000 Outdoor Leisure Series—The Dark Peak.

 Just off the main street on the western side of the village.

Early Closing Day: Wednesday.

ABOUT THE WALK - Castleton is justly famous for its caverns and castle. This walk takes you to the four caverns and descends the impressive Winnats Pass, the scene of a gruesome murder in 1788. As you return to central Castleton you can extend the outing by ascending to the ramparts of Peveril Castle or exploring the attractive parish church. The village has several inns—some with legends.

WALKING INSTRUCTIONS - Return to the main road from the car-park and turn right. 200 yards later after passing the Esso station on your left, the Methodist Church on your right, turn right, as footpath signposted beside the house named "Fair Holme". Follow the well-defined and stiled path towards Mam Tor. After 1/4 mile cross the Dunscar Farm road via the cattle grid and continue ahead, guided by the yellow-topped posts. Walk in front of a farm before bearing right up the slope to the next stile. Continue on a good path to a small plantation and crushing circle before gaining the road. Turn left and descend slowly to the entrance steps to Treak Cliff Cavern. Ascend these to the cavern and follow the public footpath beyond as you ascend the slope. The path is defined and brings you to Blue John Cavern.

On the other side ascend a stile and bear left following the path to Winnats Head Farm. Turn left at the footpath sign in front of the building to the stile. Descend the road through Winnats Pass to Speedwell Cavern. Just beyond, as footpath signed, follow the path back to Castleton. Little over 1/2 mile later reach a track via a gate beside Goosehill Hall. Descend to Goosehill Bridge; just before, you can turn right and follow the path between the houses to visit Peak Cavern. Cross the bridge and ascend to the Market Place and Youth Hostel, passing Douglas House on your left. At the Market Place you can decide whether to ascend to Peveril Castle or turn left down Castle Street to the church and inns. Turn left at the bottom and descend Cross Street back to the car park.

HISTORICAL NOTES IN WALKING ORDER

CRUSHING CIRCLE—Dates from the mid-19th Century, and although used by Odin Mine just across the road it was used by others who brought ore to be crushed from several miles away. The crusher is 18 feet in diameter, 15 inches wide, 2 inches thick, and made from eight segments. The gritstone wheel is shod by a 2 inch thick iron tyre originally held in place by wooden wedges.

ODIN MINE—Said to have been used since Roman times, but nothing recorded until 1663 . Lead ore was extracted in the 1 8th Century at the rate of as much as 800 tons a year.

TREAK CLIFF CAVERN—Show cave opened to the public in 1935. Inside are some of the finest sights of stalactites and stalagmites to be seen in Britain. Equally impressive is the display of Blue John Stone, the only place in the world where it is found.

BLUE JOHN CAVERN—Numerous examples of Blue John Stone in its natural state. Originally, large pieces were mined for making vases, as can be seen at Chatsworth House. Today only small quantities are mined for making jewellry. The stone is a rare variety of fluorspar (calcium fluoride) and generally is found in veins of about 3 inches thick. The distinctive colouring is believed to be caused by iron, manganese dioxide, asphalt or bitumen.

WINNATS MURDER—It is said that in 1758 a couple known as Alan and Clara were on their way from Castleton to Peak Forest to be married. During their stay in Castleton a miner noticed the large amount of money Alan had. He told some others, and five miners hid in the Pass and awaited them. There they coldbloodedly murdered them and stole the money. The two bodies were thrown down an old shaft. The five were never convicted but all met strange deaths, and the last to die told the gruesome story on his deathbed many years later.

SPEEDWELL CAVERN—The shop contains a few relics of lead mining, and the saddle believed to have been on Clara's horse. The cavern is a former lead mine which ceased operating in 1790. To explore the spacious caverns you first have to go by boat for half a mile along a subterranean tunnel.

PEAK CAVERN—The largest cavern entrance in Britain, being 120 feet wide and 60 feet high. The remains of a rope-making concern lie on the entrance floor. Numerous large caverns can be explored.

PEVERIL CASTLE—Known as the Castle of the Peak, the remains date from Norman times. The prominent keep was built in 1157 at a cost of £135. The castle never saw a battle and in the 16th Century was rarely used except as a jail.

PARISH CHURCH—Dedicated to St. Edmund. Dates from the Norman period and has five Norman archways. The box pews date from the 17th and 18th Century and have the occupier's name carved on. The church is unusual in having an extensive library, which was used by the villagers. Included arc two rare bibles—Cranmer's Bible dated 1539 and a Breeches Bible dated 1611.

CASTLE HOTEL—According to legend it has been haunted by a lady ghost. In 1603 a woman's body was buried under the stone doorstep.

GARLAND CEREMONY—On May 29th annually is held this ceremony in memory of the restoration of Charles II in 1660. The garland king rides on horseback encased in a 60 Ib. conical flower garland. This is later hoisted to the top of the church tower.

CHRISTMAS LIGHTS—A more recent custom has seen the main street of Castleton festooned with Christmas trees and lights—from mid-November to January 6th.

✪✪✪✪✪✪✪✪✪

CRUSHING CIRCLE - ODIN MINE

11

CASTLETON, CAVE DALE & THE WINNATS - 5 MILES

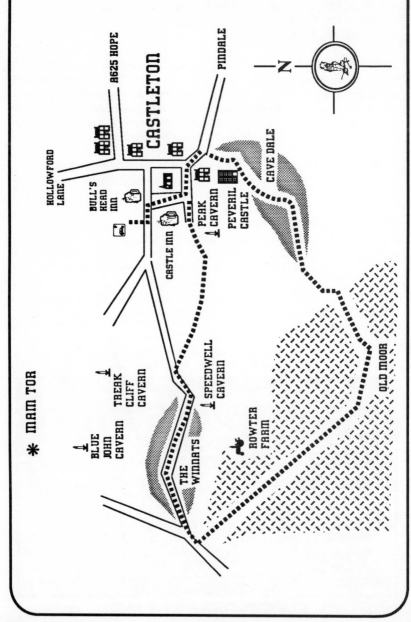

CASTLETON, CAVE DALE AND THE WINNATS - 5 MILES

- allow 2 1/2 hours.

•➤ ▬• ➤• *-Castleton - Cave Dale - Old Moor - Rowter Farm - Winnats Pass - Speedwell Cavern - Castleton.*

 - 1:25,000 Outdoor Leisure Series - The Dark Peak.

- Just off the main street on the western side of the village.

ABOUT THE WALK - After walking through the Market Place you reach Cave Dale, a magnificent limestone dale beneath Peveril Castle. You ascend out of the dale with extensive views over the castle and Hope Valley onto Old Moor. Views of Mam Tor and the northern limestone area unfold as you head towards the Winnats Pass. The pass, which you descend, is steep and dramatic and the scene of a gruesome 18th century murder. At the bottom is Speedwell Cavern; a subterrean journey into a limestone cave system. The final mile back to Castleton is beneath the valley side back to Peveril Castle and the impressive Peak Cavern.

WALKING INSTRUCTIONS - Turn left out of the car park and by the Bull's Head Inn turn right into Cross Street, past the Castle Inn. Bear left at the Youth Hostel on your right, into the Market Place, which you exit via it top lefthand corner - the Pindale Road. In a few yards turn right inbetween Dale and Cavedale Cottages and begin walking along the path into Cave Dale. Keep on the wide path past the limestone buttresses and ramparts of Peveril Castle on your right. The path begins a steep rocky ascent up the dale. At the end of the main ascent you pass through a metal gate and follow the path to your right along the shallow dale floor with a wall on your left. The dale bears left to a metal gate and stile. Cross this to the next stile and soon after bear left along a track to end the gentle ascent at a stile before a walled track and crossroads of paths on Old Moor.

Turn right along the track - signposted Winnats 1 mile. In 250 yards follow the track round to your right and in 1/2 mile pass the entrance to Rowter Farm. Continue on the track which becomes tarmaced and in another 1/2 mile reach the B6061 road. Turn right and in a few yards keep straight ahead and begin descending the Winnats Pass road. In 3/4 mile pass Speedwell Cavern on your right. Just afterwards turn right at the stile and footpath sign and follow the well defined path by the wall on your left back to Castleton. In just over 1/2 mile reach a gate and continue descending a lane to Goosehill Bridge over Peakshole Water; on your right is Peak Cavern. Cross the bridge and turn left along the path with the water on your left. Pass a cafe and reach the Buxton Road. Opposite to your right is the car park.

❄❄❄❄❄❄❄

PEVERIL CASTLE, PEAK CAVERN & GOOSEHILL HALL

THE WINNATS PASS

MAM TOR FROM NR. WINNATS HEAD FARM

TRACK ONTO STANAGE EDGE - HIGH NEB IN DISTANCE.

CASTLETON & MAM TOR - 5 MILES

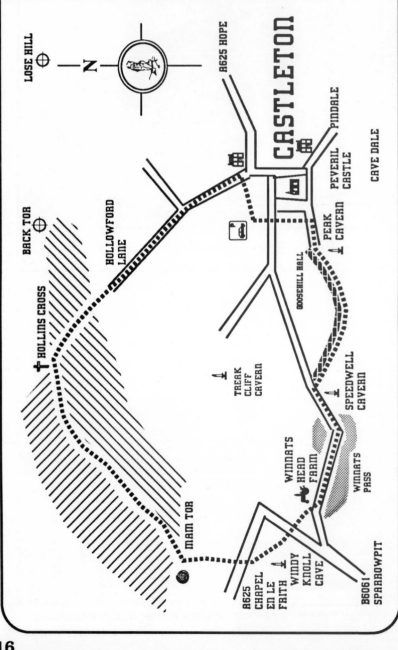

CASTLETON & MAM TOR
- 5 Miles - ALLOW 2 1/2 HOURS.

⬤⬤ ⬤⬤ ⬤⬤ - *Castleton - Speedwell Cavern - Winnats Pass - Mam Tor - Hollins Cross - Castleton.*

 - *1:25,000 Outdoor Leisure Series - The Dark Peak.*

- *Just off the main street on the western side of the village.*

ABOUT THE WALK - Castleton is famed for its lofty castle, Blue John stone and spectacular caverns full of stalagmites. This walk takes you past two of them - Peak Cavern with the largest cave entrance in Britain, and Speedwell Cavern reached by underground boat. Here you ascend the dramatic Winnats Pass, scene of a brutal murder in the 1750's. Further ascending finally brings you to the summit of Mam Tor, around which can be seen the single ditch of an Iron Age fort. The view is worth the effort, for it is 360 degrees over the limestone and moorland country of the Peak District. To the north is Kinder Scout and eastwards the Hope Valley. From the summit it is descending all the way, first along the Peakland Ridge to Hollins Cross, then more steeply at first down to Castleton.

WALKING INSTRUCTIONS - Return to the main road from the car Park and cross over to your right to gain a path beside the stream from Peak Cavern. At the end at the small road turn right over the bridge and ascend the road which soon becomes a track. Keep the wall on your right - on the other side is Goosehill Hall - and follow the defined path beside the wall as it curves right to the Winnats Pass road, 1/2 mile away. At the road turn left and ascend past Speedwell Cavern and continue up the Pass to Winnats Head Farm 1/2 mile away. Just before the farm leave the road at the stile and walk past the buildings on your left and in less than 1/4 mile reach the B6061 road. Cross over to the next stile and follow the path diagonally to your right to another stile and the A625 road. Go across to the stile opposite and ascend to the next stile in front of the road beneath Mam Tor. Just ahead on your right is the path and final ascent to Mam Tor.

After admiring the view, begin descending the Peakland Ridge and in 3/4 mile gain the circular monument at Hollins Cross. Take the path to the right which diagonally descends the slope, and in more than 1/4 mile at the end of the main descent gain a lane Hollowford Lane. Follow this for the next mile towards Castleton and shortly after entering the village outskirts, turn right to the car park.

LOSE HILL - 5 1/2 MILES

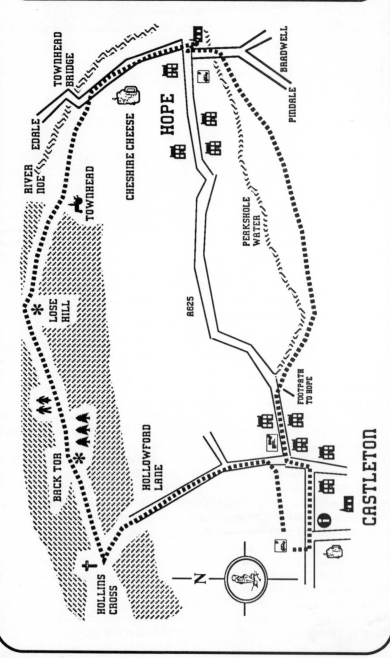

TOWNHEAD BRIDGE

RIVER NOE EDALE

CHESHIRE CHEESE

HOPE

TOWNHEAD

BRADWELL

PINDALE

PEAKSHOLE WATER

A625

LOSE HILL

BACK TOR

HOLLOWFORD LANE

FOOTPATH TO HOPE

CASTLETON

HOLLINS CROSS

N

LOSE HILL - 5 1/2 miles
- allow 2 1/2 hours
- starting from either Castleton or Hope.

O.S. MAP - *1:25,000 Outdoor Leisure Map - The Dark Peak*

- *West side of Castleton village. A further car park at Hope just west of the church.*

- *Castleton - Peakshole Water - Hope - Back Tor - Hollins Cross - Hollowford Road - Castleton.*

ABOUT THE WALK - Starting from the Peak District's most famous village, you traverse the floor of the Hope Valley to Hope before ascending Lose Hill. From this vantage point you can survey much of the mountainous region of the National Park. Next follows a delightful ridge walk before descending back to the valley floor. You can also start this walk from Hope.

WALKING INSTRUCTIONS - From the large car park on the western side of Castleton village walk through the village to the eastern side. There is much to be explored in Castleton, such as Peak Cavern, the church, and Peveril Castle, but leave these as your reward until the end ! Before you get to the road bridge over Peakshole Water turn right along a small lane signposted for Hope. For a short distance you walk down the walled lane before leaving it and crossing the fields towards Hope, with the water flowing on your left.

Just over a mile later you gain the minor road on the South side of Hope village. Turn left and ascend into the village. As you do so on your immediate left is a splendid example of a village pinfold. Hope church you pass on your right and if open it is well worth exploring. The churchyard contains a Saxon cross shaft. The church is mainly 13th. century and contains the tombs to two 'Wood reeves' of the Royal Forest of the Peak. In the chancel are Jacobean pews and panelling with the arms of the Eyre and Beresford families. Nearby is the Jacobean pulpit and a schoolmaster's chair dated 1664 with a Latin motto meaning *'You cannot make a scholar out of a block of wood'*. The parish records contains one of the few entries in Derby

-shire of body snatching—'1831, October 26th aged 28, William Bradwell, Smalldale. The body stolen same night'.

From the church, cross the A625 road (Hope car park is on your left) and walk along the road signposted for Edale. Almost a mile along here and shortly before the road crosses the river Noe, turn left along a lane. At the junction 200 yards later, turn left towards the farm, Townhead. Almost immediately afterwards turn right and ascend the sunken wooded track. Minutes later you leave the foliage behind emerging into open country as you begin the steady climb up the broad shoulder to the summit of Lose Hill. There is only one way to ascend a hill and that is to adopt a steady pace and don't stop until you reach the top. You will be surprised how soon you get there ! When you stand on the top and view the panorama at your feet, the effort is soon forgotten.

From the valley you will have ascended just under 1,000 ft to 1,563 ft. Northwards your eyes gaze over Kinder, Bleaklow and the Derwent valley, while immediately below is the Vale of Edale. Southwards is the Hope Valley and the moors of Offerton and Bradwell. Looking South West the next 1 1/4 miles of the walk can be seen along the Peakland Ridge to Back Tor and Hollins Cross. Dominating the far end is Mam Tor and its Iron Age fort. The walk along the ridge with captivating views on either side, has few equals in Derbyshire. After Back Tor you descend steeply before continuing along the ridge to the meeting of the paths at Hollins Cross. Here you turn left and begin descending towards Castleton.

After half a mile and at the base of the ridge you join a farm road known as Hollowford Road and continue along it for the final mile back to Castleton. As you enter the village the car park is on your right. Now having walked in both the valley and heights of the vicinity you can enjoy the treasures of Castleton. The church is aisleless and contains box pews, a splendid Norman chancel arch, several old Bibles and a unique church library. A short walk from here brings you to Peak Cavern, the second largest cavern entrance in the world. The interior contains five rope walks, now sadly abandoned, but they were in continuous use for 500 years. Towering above all is Peveril Castle and its prominent keep, built in 1176 for £135!

The walk completed and Castleton explored, you can return home full of rich sights and knowledge after experiencing a rewarding day.

START OF PATH FROM CASTLETON TO HOPE VIA PEAKSHOLE WATER.

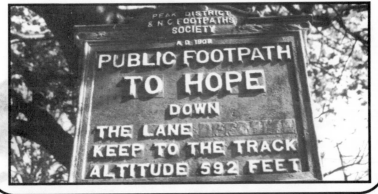

PEAK DISTRICT
& N C FOOTPATHS
SOCIETY
A D 1902
PUBLIC FOOTPATH
TO HOPE
DOWN
THE LANE
KEEP TO THE TRACK
ALTITUDE 592 FEET

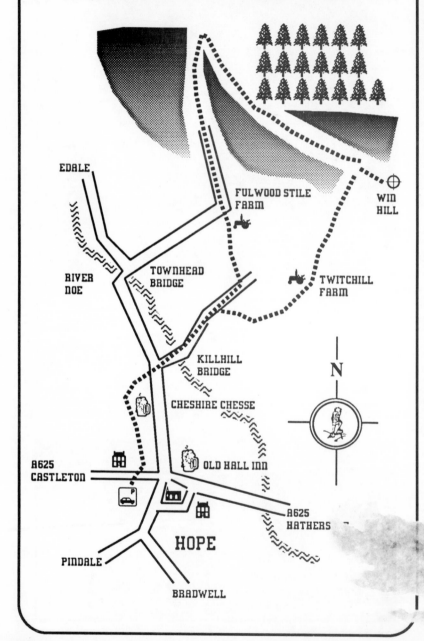

WIN HILL - 6 MILES
SOUTHERN ROUTE

EDALE

FULWOOD STILE FARM

WIN HILL

RIVER NOE

TOWNHEAD BRIDGE

TWITCHILL FARM

KILLHILL BRIDGE

CHESHIRE CHESSE

N

A625 CASTLETON

OLD HALL INN

A625 HATHERS

HOPE

PINDALE

BRADWELL

HOPE - WIN HILL - 6 MILES
Southern route - allow 2 1/2 hours.

⬤⬤ ⬤⬤ ⬤⬤ *- Hope - Killhill - Fulwood Stile Farm - Win Hill - Twitchill*

Farm - Killhill - Hope.

O.S. MAP *- 1:25,000 Outdoor Leisure Map - The Dark Peak.*

- Central Hope, just off the A625 road, at Grid Ref. SK172835.

ABOUT THE WALK - Win Hill has a rocky ridged summit from where one of the finest views in the Peak District unfolds. The walk takes you gently up the slopes of the hill on a 1,000 foot ascent. The descent is steep but impressive. Take your sandwiches and sit on the summit and soak up the view to Kinder, Bleaklow and the reservoirs of the Derwent Valley. Southwards is the Hope Valley and gritstone edges.

WALKING INSTRUCTIONS - From the car park entrance turn right and left almost immediately past the Blacksmith's Cottage onto the footpath signed path - Lose Hill. Plaque No. 68. The path, which is well stiled, passes between the houses, across a small housing estate. At the end of the next field turn right through two stiles and descend the field to the road at Killhill. On your right , is a large white House. You will retrace this part of the route on your way back. Cross the Edale road and descend the minor road crossing Killhill Bridge over the River Noe. Keep on the road bearing left at the junction and pass under the railway line. Follow the road round to your left and where it turns right keep straight ahead and cross three fields to Fulwood Stile Farm. Walk through the farm to the road . Keep ahead and begin ascending gently. In a 1/3 mile keep right and ascend more steeply on a track. At the top where it levels out after nearly 1/2 mile of ascent, turn right and follow the wide defined path to the summit of Win Hill 1 1/2 miles away.

Descend from the summit the way you came for a 1/3 mile. At the third mound of stones turn left along the wide path and begin the gradual, then steep, descent to the ruins of Twitchill Farm. At the top of the steep section you reach a crossroads of paths. Keep straight ahead - Hope 3/4 mile. From the farm you descend a track, which after 1/4 mile bears right and passes under the Manchester railway. Here turn left and descend the now tarmaced lane back to Killhill and your starting our path. Retrace your steps back to Hope.

WIN HILL - 1,518 feet/462 metres - The 360 degree spectacular view has few equals in the Peak District. According to ancient legend, the hill and the other opposite - Lose Hill - was the scene of a battle in the 7th century. The opposing armies occupied the hills. The next day the armies descended and the battle raged in the valley below. The River Noe is reputed to have turned crimson. At the end of the day the battle was over. The winner's hill where they camped became known as Win Hill, and the losers' - Lose Hill!

HOPE CHURCH - Dedicated to St. Peter and dates from the early 15th century. Inside are grave slabs, Jacobean pews, and a coat of arms to the Eyre family who were once the principal landowners in the area. The schoolmaster's chair has a Latin inscription on it meaning - *"You cannot make a scholar out of a block of wood."*

❋❋❋❋❋❋❋

HOPE CHURCH

24

RIVER NOE FROM KILLHILL BRIDGE

DAGGERS HOUSE, NEAR HOPE CHURCH

WIN HILL - 8 MILES
NORTHERN ROUTE

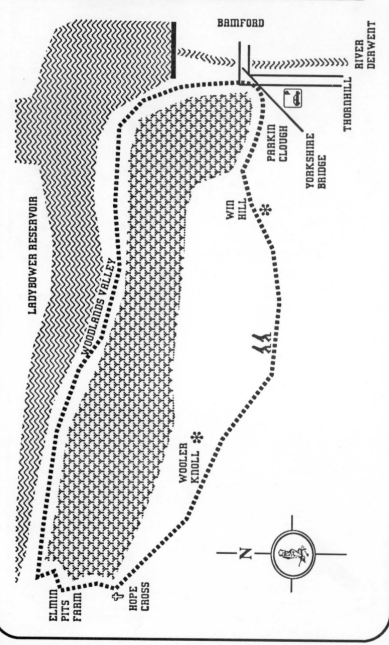

BAMFORD

RIVER DERWENT

THORNHILL

PARKIN CLOUGH

YORKSHIRE BRIDGE

WIN HILL

LADYBOWER RESERVOIR

WOODLANDS VALLEY

WOOLER KNOLL

ELMIN PITS FARM

HOPE CROSS

N

WIN HILL - 8 miles - NORTHERN ROUTE - allow 3 1/2 hours.

  - *Yorkshire Bridge - Ladybower Reservoir - Woodlands Valley - Elmin Pits Farm - Hope Cross - Wooler Knoll - Win Hill - Parkin Clough - Yorkshire Bridge.*

O.S. MAP - *1:25,000 Outdoor Leisure Map - "The Dark Peak".*

P - *roadside parking at Yorkshire Bridge.*

ABOUT THE WALK - I never tire of ascending Win Hill and admiring the sweeping panorama that unfolds from her summit. The view really is exceptional. To get there this circular walk takes you through wooded country and beside one of the largest reservoirs in Derbyshire. The actual ascent is gradual and within half an hour of the summit you should be back at the Yorkshire Bridge, for the descent is direct. It is one of those walks that can be enjoyed at any season; in winter you see the snow-capped tops of Bleaklow and Kinder and in the summer you see the rich colours shimmering against the blue waters of the reservoirs.

WALKING INSTRUCTIONS - From the Yorkshire Bridge turn right and head northwards along the road on the left-hand side of Ladybower Reservoir. After a few yards you will see the signpost and steps to Win Hill. These you will descend later. For the moment keep straight ahead and follow the nearest track to the head of the reservoir, about 3l miles. It is delightful walking for you pass the dam wall of Ladybower Reservoir which was completed in 1945. It is 140 feet high, 1,250 feet long and 665 feet thick at its base, tapering to 17 feet at the top. Work began on the reservoir in 1935 and during the ten years of construction more than 100,000 tons of clay and 1,000,000 tons of earth were moved. The surface area of the reservoir is 504 acres and has a holding capacity of 6,300 million gallons.

During construction several farms and two villages were evacuated and demolished. Some you will see on the walk. After the first three-quarters of a mile you can look across at Ashopton viaduct. Basically beneath it are the ruins of the village of Ashopton. A mile later you pass the ruins of Nether Ashop on your right, while across the water are the rocky outcrops of Crook Hill. At the head of the reservoir opposite a small road junction on the A57 are the remains of a lorry trailer. Behind it is the track, on your left, going diagonally to the right through the pine trees. Turn left here and ascend through the trees to the ruins of Elmin Pits Farm, a little over a quarter of a mile away.

At the ruins turn sharp left and continue ascending on a small track to the ridge and Hope Cross. The cross bears the date 1737 but is believed to be older. On its four sides can be seen the place names of *Hope*, *Glossop*, *Edale* and *Sheffield*. Passing by it is the course of an old Roman Road which formerly linked the Roman fort of Navio near Brough to Melandra near Glossop. Follow the wide track here and descend slightly to a gate. Just past the gate turn left along the well-trodden path and begin the gradual ascent to the summit of Win Hill two miles away. This is magnificent walking with views on your right to the Edale valley, Lose Hill and the ridge to Mam Tor, the Hope valley and across the valley to Shatton and Abney Moor. When you gain the rocky summit, 1,518 feet, you can also look down towards Hathersage and the gritstone edges of Bamford, Stanage and Mill-stone.

According to tradition, in 630 A.D. there was a battle here between Edwin, King of Northumbria, and Cynegils and Cuichelm, the Kings of Wessex. Edwin was on the scene first and so camped around the summit of Win Hill. The Kings of Wessex arrived the following day and camped on Lose Hill. The next day the battle raged and by nightfall Edwin was the winner. As a result his hill was known as Win Hill and the Wessex's hill as Lose Hill !

Having fully absorbed the view from the summit triangulation pillar, especially northwards to the Ashopton viaduct and across to the Derwent Moorlands, descend due east, thereby traversing the moun-tain. The path is distinct and once through the ladder stile over the wall, keep straight ahead. Continue straight ahead to a stone wall in the trees . Here turn right and left almost immediately afterwards and begin to descend Parkin Clough. The path is just on the left-hand side of the stream beside a wall - it is steep - so take your time. At the bottom go down the steps to the Win Hill path sign you passed at the beginning of the walk. Turn right on gaining the track and a few more strides bring you to the Yorkshire Bridge. There you should glow with pride at ascending one of The Peak District's finest view points.

WIN HILL'S ROCKY SUMMIT.

VIEW FROM WIN HILL'S SUMMIT TO ASHOPTON VIADUCT
OVER LADYBOWER RESERVOIR.

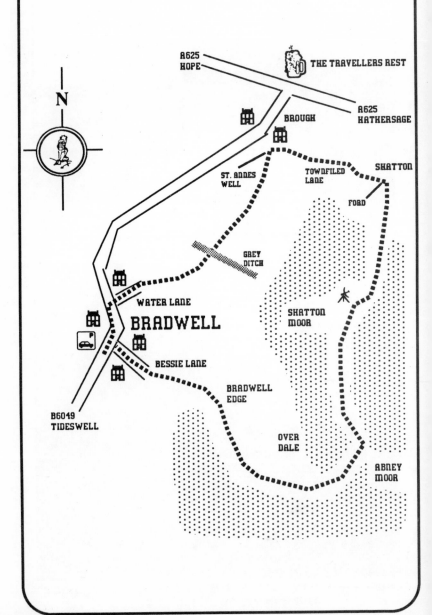

SHATTON MOOR - 6 MILES

N

A625
HOPE

THE TRAVELLERS REST

BROUGH

A625
HATHERSAGE

ST. ANNES
WELL

TOWNFIELD
LANE

SHATTON

FORD

GREY
DITCH

SHATTON
MOOR

WATER LANE

BRADWELL

BESSIE LANE

BRADWELL
EDGE

B6049
TIDESWELL

OVER
DALE

ABNEY
MOOR

SHATTON MOOR - 6 miles - allow 2 1/4 hours.

Bradwell - Grey Ditch - Brough - Townfield Lane - Shatton - Shatton Lane- Shatton Moor- Bradwell Edge - Bradwell Hills - Bradwell.

- I :25,000 Outdoor Leisure Map- 'The Dark Peak'

Central Bradwell.

ABOUT THE WALK - The first part of this walk is through limestone country before reaching the Hope Valley and gritstone country. From Shatton there is a gradual ascent onto magnificent moorland before descending over Bradwell Edge to Bradwell, taking a path, which in my opinion, gives one of the most impressive descents into a valley, with breathtaking views and several interesting items of past history to be encountered on the way.

WALKING INSTRUCTIONS - From the car park turn left and immediately after crossing Bradwell Brook, turn right down Water Lane. One hundred yards later, bear right through the stile beside the signpost and begin crossing the fields to Brough a mile away: the path line is faint but all the limestone stiles are there. After a short distance you walk over the defence earthwork- Grey Ditch - which can be seen very clearly here. Almost three quarters of a mile later you descend to the houses of Brough. Do not turn left to the B6049 turn right for Shatton opposite St. Anne Cottage where a road sign states 'Unsuitable for Motors'. St Anne's well is situated on the corner and bears the date 1859.

Keep to the road (which later deteriorates into a track), and gradually ascend the slope, ignoring the road to your right up Rebellion Knoll. Here, as indicated by the footpath signpost, follow the track beside the hedge to your right; you are now walking along Townfield Lane. The lane sides are steep and during Spring and early Summer are ablaze with flowers - primula, lesser celandine and red campion. Almost a mile from Brough you reach the ford at Shatton. The footpath bridge is on the left-hand side. On meeting the road on the other side, turn right and begin the gradual steady ascent to the summit of Shatton Moor. The television mast is what you are heading for and the lane, although bearing no name plate, is known as

Shatton Lane. At first it is tarmacadamed but deteriorates to a grassy track. The air is pure and the skylarks sing - ah! the joys of being out in the countryside.

The track curves round the hillside beneath the summit of Abney Moor. The television mast is a tantalising vantage point and although you seem at times to be walking away from it you do eventually reach it. Behind you a superb view unfolds as you climb higher, with Win Hill below and the Hope Valley to your left and right. Continue past the mast and turn sharp right to keep on the track around the head of Over Dale, ignoring all the tracks on your left to Abney. On the walk round the head of the valley you pass a sign saying 'Bradwell 1 1/4 miles' so you haven't far to go! On the other side of the valley and just where the track begins to drop down past Rebellion Knoll to Brough, is a gate across the track: on the other side and to the left is the stile and path to Bradwell. Simply keep the gritstone wall on your left and the stiles will be found at the field ends. At the end of the second field a stunning view of Bradwell unfolds. The path, which follows an old packhorse route, is partly paved. You descend diagonally to your right; part way down turn left and then right to gain the lane down into Bradwell, keeping straight ahead to Bessie Lane. Here the road divides with a row of cottages in the middle. Take the right fork and turn right again down into Bradwell. This row of cottages was formerly a small business where Bradda Hats were made in the 18th century. The industry started in Bradwell in the 17th century and Job Middleton, the last hatter, died in 1899 aged 84. The hats, which were dome-shaped with a brim, are known to have been quite serviceable for more than 200 years and were worn mostly in the lead mines. The tin hats used in World War One were styled on their pattern.

As you walk into central Bradwell, opposite the church can be seen a cottage on your left, where Samuel Fox was born in June 1815. He used to work in a needle factory in Hathersage and to get there he cycled on a bike which he called 'the bone shaker'. Samuel Fox went on to invent the Paragon umbrella frame and was the founder of the now huge Stocksbridge works near Sheffield. The car park is not far away from where the walk ends.

ST. ANNE'S WELL, BROUGH, DATED 1859.

THE DESCENT INTO BRADWELL - FOLLOWS THE WALL.

HATHERSAGE VILLAGE WALK - 3 MILES

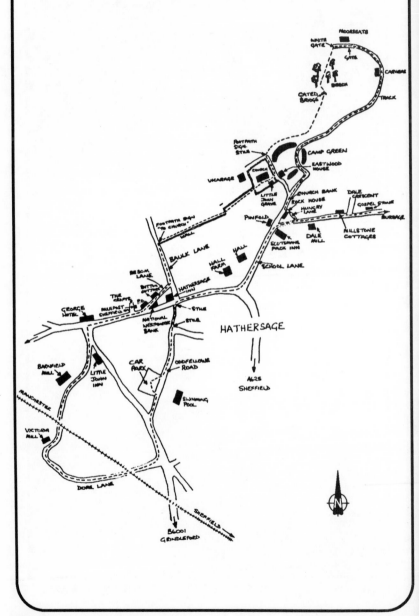

HATHERSAGE VILLAGE WALK
- 3 Miles - ALLOW 2 HOURS

 1:25,000 Pathfinder Series—Sheffield—Sheet No. SK 28/38.

 Oddfellows Road—just off the B6001 Grindleford Road

Early Closing Day: Wednesday.

ABOUT THE WALK - Hathersage is extremely rich in local and national history. Many old buildings and industries remain, and on this walk you reach numerous places of interest and ascend above the village to admire its setting. On the walk you will pass old needle and button factories, see Little John's Grave, explore a magnificent 14th Century church, see exquisite brasses to the Eyre family, a Hall linked to Charlotte Bronte's novel—Jane Eyre—and see the village pinfold and pass numerous pubs!

WALKING INSTRUCTIONS - Turn right out of the car-park down Oddfellows Road to the Grindleford (B6001) road. Turn left, and 50 yards later right down Dore Lane. Follow this lane round passing under two railway arches and past the Victoria Mill and Barnfield Mill, before regaining the Grindleford road with the Little John Inn on your right. Turn left and right almost immediately onto the main street, the A625 road. 150 yards later walk up Besom Lane with the Post office on your left and the National Westminster Bank on your right. At the top turn left along Baulk Lane. 100 yards later turn right, as footpath signposted, and ascend the path to the church.

Pass through the Lynch Gate and turn left. 30 yards later turn right at the footpath sign and stile. Follow the curvature of the fence on your right to near a metal stile. Here bear left on a well-defined path which descends to a gated bridge. Cross and follow the path as it ascends through the beech trees to Moorseats Hall. Turn right at the white gate and pass through another gate shortly afterwards before gaining the track. Follow the track round to your right, past Carhead House, before descending gradually towards Camp Green and the metal stile you saw earlier. Follow the road as it zig-zags through Camp Green before reaching Church Bank. Descend another 20 yards before turning sharp left down a path into Hungry Lane .

Turn left and walk up the road to see Dale Mill, Millstone Cottages and the Gospel Stone. Retrace your steps and continue along School Lane to the A625 road. Turn right and 150 yards later, opposite the Hathersage Inn, turn left through a stone stile and regain, another 50 yards later, Oddfellows Road. Continue ahead back to the Car Park.

HISTORICAL NOTES - IN WALKING ORDER

VICTORIA MILL— Long single-storey buildings dating back to early last century. Originally used for the manufacture of cast steel wire and hackle pins. Later used for the manufacture of gramophone needles.

BARNFIELD MILL — From the mid-18th Century to late 19th Century Hathersage was a major producer of needles. At this mill Samuel Fox was an apprentice in 1815 and he later moved to Stocksbridge, near Sheffield, and started the now large steel works there. Another needle mill is Dale Mill, and a tunnel goes under the road to Eastwood Cottages and is believed to have been used for wire drawing.

MILEPOST—At the entrance to "The Crofts" an old milepost—Sheffield 10 miles—can be seen.

BUTTONS—An old three-storey building on Besom Lane, near the Post Office, was built, as the circular plaque details, by the Furniss family in 1781. The industry was short-lived, and in 1820 was described as "declining".

PARISH CHURCH—Dedicated to St. Michael's. The church largely dates from the late 14th Century, and is very closely associated with the Eyre family and Little John. The Eyre family were major landowners in the Hope Valley—more than 20,000 acres. In the 16th Century they built many fine Halls nearby—North Lees, Moorseats, Highlow and Offerton. Inside are several brasses to the Eyre family dating back to 1643.

LITTLE JOHN GRAVE—Robin Hood's faithful companion is reputed to be buried here. In 1784 the grave was excavated and a thigh bone 29 1/2 inches long was found—which would mean that Little John was eight foot tall. For many years Little John's cap and how hung in the church. An inn in the village recalls his name, and two miles away, on Stanage Edge, Robin Hood's Cave recalls his companion .

MOORSEATS—Built by the Eyre family in the 16th Century. In 1845 Charlotte Bronte stayed in Hathersage at the vicarage; the vicar being Henry Nussey, the brother of her close friend Ellen Nussey. While she was here she visited the surrounding area and later wrote her famous novel Jane Eyre. Many of the places in the book have been identified with the area—Morton is Hathersage; Moorseats is Moor House where the Rivers' sister lived; and North Lees Hall is Thornfeld Hall.

CAMP GREEN—An earthwork sometimes known as Danes Camp, dating from the 9th Century.

GOSPEL STONE—The large stone is now part of a wall, but a plaque records its importance. Here on the Rogation Service, when walking the boundaries of the parish, the vicar would stand on the stone and offer prayers.

PINFOLD—One of the few left in Derbyshire. Here last century any straying animals were locked in until ownership was established. The owner then had to pay a fine to the parish before the animal was released.

SCOTSMAN'S PACK INN—An inn has occupied this site since the 14th Century; this one dates from 1912. As the inn sign portrays, the inn was on a major packhorse route—from Hathersage to Longshaw and on to Sheffield, and another via Stanage Pole to Sheffield. Inside is Little John's chair.

HATHERSAGE INN—Originally known as the Ordnance Arms, it was built by Major A.A. Shuttleworth in 1808.

LITTLE JOHN'S TOMBSTONE

OFFERTON MOOR - 10 MILES

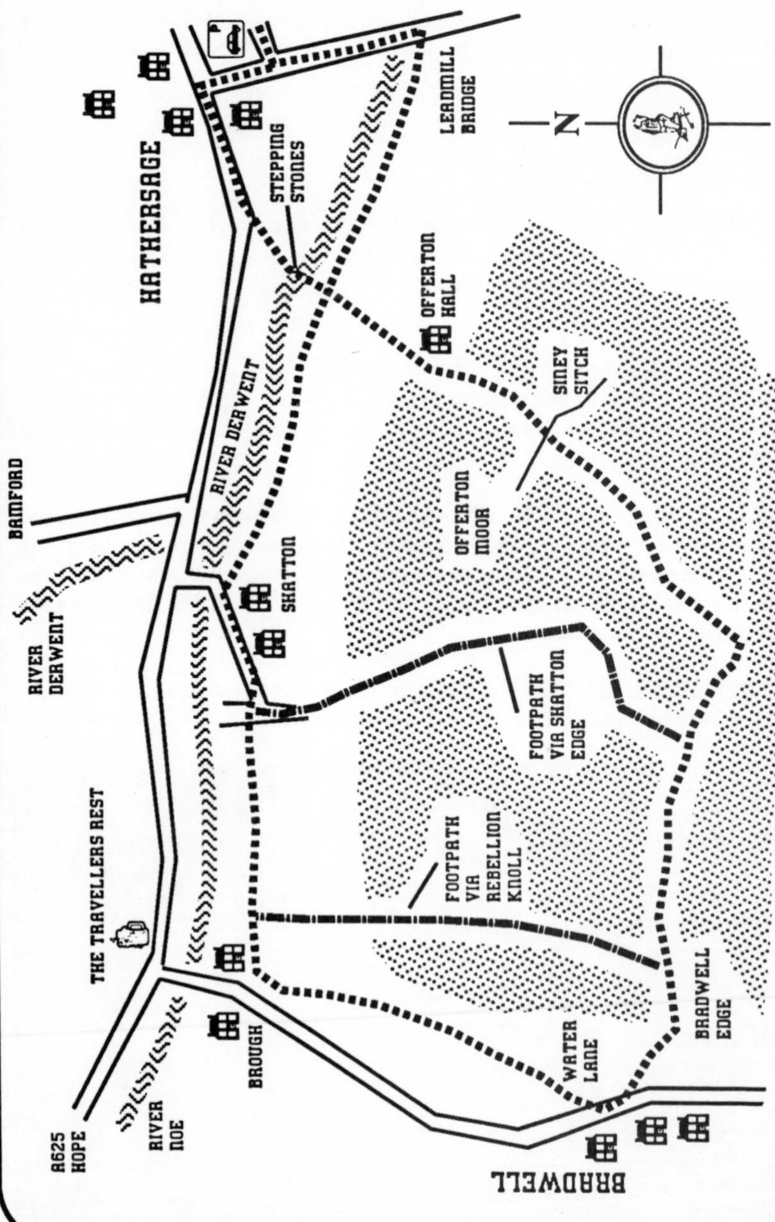

OFFERTON MOOR - 10 miles - allow 3 1/2 hours. Can be shortened to 6 or 8 miles.

 - *1:25,000 Pathfinder Series - Sheet No. SK 28/38 - Sheffield.*
- *1:25,000 Outdoor Leisure Map - The Dark Peak.*

 - *Opposite Swimming Pool in Hathersage.*

- Hathersage - Offerton Hall - Offerton Moor - Bradwell Edge - Bradwell - Brough - Shatton - River Derwent - Leadmill Bridge - Hathersage.

ABOUT THE WALK - Offerton Moor has long been a favourite moorland area of mine. On New Year's day, when the valleys were murky with thick fog, I took a group of friends on this walk. On the moor we baked in hot sun falling from a blue sky and looked across at a sea of clouds. The walk is the longest in the book but I make no apologies for it is magnificent walking country. The walk can be considerably shortened for you can descend past Shatton Edge to Shatton itself. Alternatively you can go down Rebellion Knoll to Brough and omit Bradwell - making the walk about 8 miles long. Similarly you can on regaining the stepping stones retrace your steps back to Hathersage and omit Leadmill Bridge, thus making a walk of about 6 miles overall.

WALKING INSTRUCTIONS - In Hathersage descend to the main A625 road from the car park and turn left and walk along it for half a mile. On your left you will see a footpath sign and stone stile; turn left and go through the stile and descend the field to the river Derwent. A short distance along here you reach the curving stepping stones across the river. Cross the river and as signposted ascend the fields to the walled lane in front of Offerton Hall, half a mile away. Go on past the hall and on rounding a sharp right-hand bend, you will find, on your right, the wooden stile and path onto the summit of Offerton Moor. At first you ascend directly before bearing right up a ditch. The pathline is well defined and once on the moorland there is no more climbing on the remainder of the walk. Now you enjoy the reward of your labour for the moor provides a good vantage point over the Hope Valley to Kinder and to Hucklow and Eyam Moor.

Follow the path across the moorland and after half a mile you cross Siney Sitch. Half a mile later you begin descending towards Abney. After a very short distance turn right and follow another path which soon hugs the right-hand side of a wall as you begin making your way to the track across Shatton Moor, three quarters of a mile away. At the track turn left and walk along it for the next three quarters of a mile. As you walk along, Abney village is to your left and on your right is the shallow Over Dale After 3/4 mile the track begins to descend to Rebellion Knoll. Here, go through the first gate you come to and immediately ascend the stone stile on your left. Follow the path keeping the wall on your left and in less than a quarter of a mile you reach Bradwell Edge. Here the path descends steeply to Bradwell via Bradwell Hills. The view from here over the Hope Valley to Mam Tor and Kinder must rate as one of the finest viewpoints in the Peak District. It is a stunning scene.

Descend the path and later roads to the B6049 road in Bradwell. Turn right, walk down the road through the village, passing, on your left, the cottage where Samuel Fox was born in 1815. He invented the paragon umbrella frame and his works is now the huge complex in the valley at Stocksbridge. Just after his cottage turn right along a lane with the brook on your immediate left. After about 200 yards turn right through a stone stile and begin crossing the fields to Brough one and a quarter miles away. The pathline is faint but the stone stiles act as guide lines. After half a mile cross a couple of tracks and then after a further half mile descend to St. Anne's Cottages at Brough. You will see St. Ann's well on your right, at the junction of the track to Shatton.

Turn right and follow this signposted track to Shatton one and a quarter miles away. In a very short distance the track from Rebellion Knoll comes in from your right. Keep straight ahead, ascending slightly. Beyond, as signposted, keep to the righthand edge of the field before joining a sunken lane to Shatton and its ford. Walk past the houses of Shatton and just before the bridge over the river Derwent, turn right through the stile and follow the well defined path beside the river. The river on your left is your companion for the next one and a quarter miles back to the stepping stones. Here you can retrace your steps to Hathersage or continue beside the river to Leadmill Bridge, one and a half miles away. There you turn left and ascend the road (B6001) into Hathersage. There, one of the most beautiful walks in the Peak District ends.

RIVER DERWENT AND LEADMILL BRIDGE.

THE PLOUGH INN, LEADMILL.

STANAGE EDGE - 5 1/2 MILES

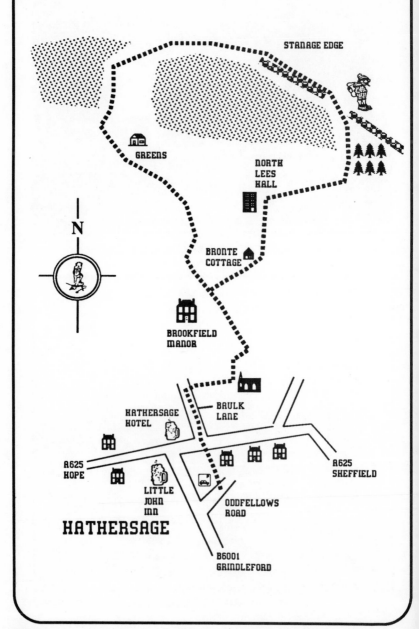

STANAGE EDGE

GREENS

NORTH LEES HALL

N

BRONTE COTTAGE

BROOKFIELD MANOR

BAULK LANE

HATHERSAGE HOTEL

A625 HOPE

LITTLE JOHN INN

HATHERSAGE

A625 SHEFFIELD

ODDFELLOWS ROAD

B6001 GRINDLEFORD

HATHERSAGE AND STANAGE EDGE - 5 1/2 Miles - allow 2 1/2 HOURS

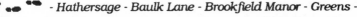 *- Hathersage - Baulk Lane - Brookfield Manor - Greens -*

 Stannage Edge - North Lees Hall - Hathersage.
- 1:25,000 Pathfinder Series Sheet No SK 28/38 - Sheffield

- Oddfellows Road - just off the B6001 Grindleford Road.

ABOUT THE WALK - Hathersage is worth exploring in its own right with its remains of a former needle industry. First you ascend to the church and see the grave to Little John, Robin Hood's faithful companion. From here you cross fields and walk past Brookfield Manor. Beyond you follow a path through woodland to Green's House and ascend to the minor road beneath Stanage Edge. You continue ascending to the Edge before descending and passing the magnificent Elizabethan tower building, North Lees Hall. The Hall features in Charlotte Bronte's novel, *"Jane Eyre"* and is described as Marsh End. You regain your earlier path and instead of going to the church continue descending back into Hathersage.

WALKING INSTRUCTIONS - Gain Oddfellows Road from the car park and turn left along it. Where it turns right keep straight ahead on a path which brings you to the main street. Cross over to your right to the righthand side of the Hathersage Inn and walk along Baulk Lane. After about 80 yards turn right at the footpath sign - To Church - and ascend to it. Walk past it on your right - the Little John Gravestone is on your right - and pass through the Lynch gate. Turn left and at the lefthand corner shortly afterwards, turn right at the stile and footpath sign. Walk along the path a few yards before turning left and descending to a small stream. Ascend gently keeping the field edge on your left for two fields then on your right to a track. Turn right along this and in about 100 yards as signed bear left on a path which keeps to the righthand side of the buildings of Brookfield Manor. Beyond reach the minor road from Stanage Edge. Cross over to the path signed - Greens. The path is defined as you soon enter woodland and in 1/4 mile cross a footbridge and ascend with a stream on your left. Pass between the buildings of Green's

House and turn right. First you curve right then left as you ascend to the minor road beneath Stanage.

Turn left and 100 yards later right and follow the curving track to the crest of Stanage Edge. Here turn right at a stile and walk along the top of the Edge for less then 1/4 mile to a path on your right. Turn right and descend this past pine trees and large gritstone boulders to the minor road and car Park. Turn left along it and in about 70 yards right down a track to North Lees. Turn left passing the building on your right and descend the tarmaced road to the minor road. Turn right and in a few yards you regain your earlier Path. Turn left and walk past Brookfield Manor, now on your right. On regaining the track turn left along it and follow it all the way back to Hathersage - Baulk Lane and the Hathersage Inn. Cross the main road - A625 - and retrace your steps back to the car park.

STANAGE EDGE - EASTERN END.

VIEW OVER BROOKFIELD PARK TO HATHERSAGE.

PADLEY CHAPEL.

PADLEY CHAPEL & LONGSHAW COUNTRY PARK - 4 MILES

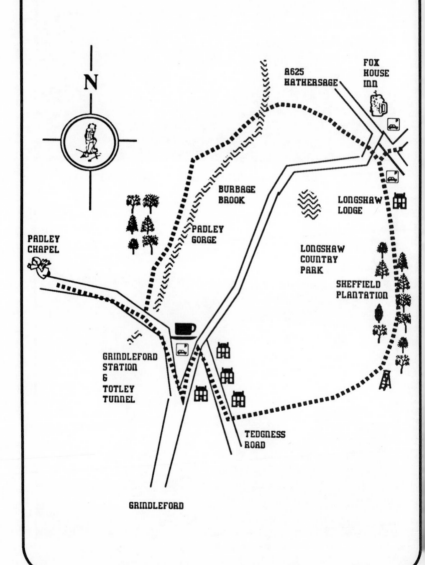

N

FOX HOUSE INN

A625 HATHERSAGE

BURBAGE BROOK

LONGSHAW LODGE

PADLEY GORGE

LONGSHAW COUNTRY PARK

PADLEY CHAPEL

SHEFFIELD PLANTATION

GRINDLEFORD STATION & TOTLEY TUNNEL

TEDGNESS ROAD

GRINDLEFORD

PADLEY CHAPEL & LONGSHAW COUNTRY PARK
- **4 miles** - allow 1 1/2 hours.

 *Fox House—Longshaw Lodge Longshaw Estate—Sheffield Plantation Nether Padley—Grindleford Station—Padley Chapel—Padley Gorge—Burbage Brook—Fox House.*

Grindleford Station and National Trust Car Park, Longshaw.

O.S. MAP - *1:25,000 Outdoor Leisure Map - The White Peak.*
- *1:25,000 Pathfinder Series Sheet No. SK28/38 - Sheffield*

ABOUT THE WALK - Distant views, rugged scenery and a martyr chapel are just three of the attractions of this walk. Coupled with this is extensive woodland, the home of a variety of birds and wild flowers. It is a walk which is as equally attractive in the summer months as the winter, and also makes an ideal Christmas outing.

FOX HOUSE - takes its name from its original builder, Mr. Fox of Callow Farm, just below Offerton Moor, dates back to the 17th century and was originally a shepherd's cottage. Later it was enlarged by various Dukes of Rutland, the adjacent Longshaw Estate being part of their shooting preserves which covered 13,000 acres. These were sold in 1927 and the Longshaw Estate became part of the National Trust in 1931, with further additions over the next five years, thanks to public subscriptions.

SHEEPDOG TRIALS - It was in Fox House Inn in 1896 that a group of shepherds met and decided to hold sheepdog trials. The first trial was planned to take place on 24th March, 1898, on Totley Moor. A snowstorm on that day caused its abandonment and it was held the following day in the field below the road to Longshaw Lodge. Since then it has proved to be a special event in Derbyshire's calendar, and is held each year at the beginning of September. The original plan was to have a pigeon shoot, but as most of the shepherds had dogs and not guns the idea was abandoned and sheepdog trials were decided upon instead.

JANE EYRE - The road junction outside Fox House is believed to be the "Whitecross" where Charlotte Bronte's "Jane Eyre" left the coach on her flight north. Regular coach traffic existed to the inn until about 1895, when the Totley tunnel was completed and the railway began operation. The inn was a frequent holiday place for Sheffield people. The sharp right-hand bend in the road at Fox House is because the Duke of Rutland would not allow it to come across his property.

WALKING INSTRUCTIONS - From Fox House go straight across the road and over a stone stile to descend a path to the road to Longshaw Lodge. On the righthand side of the road, under a tree close to the gate, is an old signpost and on each of its four sides are the road names— *"Sheffield Rode", "Dronfield Side", "Tideswell Rode", and "Hope Rode"*. Other old gritstone signposts can be seen on the Longshaw estate, but few of the roads are visible today. One from here that can be traced goes past the right-hand edge of the Longshaw pool. Follow the road towards the Lodge and after about 100 yards turn right down some stone steps to take the path round the right-hand side of the grounds. Go through the metal gate close to the chapel and the subsequent white gate, and follow the wide grass driveway through the estate for the next mile.

LONGSHAW LODGE - The actual building date of Longshaw Lodge is unknown, but it is believed to have been started in 1830. It acted as a shooting lodge for the Dukes of Rutland, who enlarged the building. The sixth duke, who died in 18X8 and was known as the "Bachelor duke" and "Sporting duke", made the various driveways through the estate. The pond appears to have been constructed at the same time as the lodge in 1830. Following the building's sale in 1927, it was for a while a guest house of the Holiday Fellowship but has now been converted into private flats.

About half a mile from the white gate you pass through Sheffield Plantation, which originally covered an area of 100 acres and was owned by a Sheffield based company formed in 1823. It was later sold to the Duke of Rutland in 1856. About half a mile later the trees thin out and the driveway curves to your left. Some 20 yards on your right is a wooden ladder stile; surmount this and descend the field which is often quite wet. At the other end of the field, cross a stream and ascend briefly to a small wood. Another ladder stile on your right takes you down through the silver birch trees. On meeting Tedgness Road at the bottom turn right, cross the main road (A6011) and descend the track on your left to Grindleford station. You are now at the halfway point and a small cafe here fortifies you for the other half!

From the cafe cross the railway bridge. On your right is the entrance to Totley tunnel, which at 3 miles 950 yards is the second longest in Britain. It was started in September 1888 and four years later it had been blasted through. On 1st June, 1894, it was of officially opened. During the course of construction, 163 tons of gelignite had been used. The cost per yard was approximately £75 and progress was estimated at about 20 yards a week. Water was a constant hazard during the tunnelling and as much as 26,000 gallons an hour pumped out. At one stage the figure rose to over five million gallons a day.

Once over the bridge bear left past Padley Mill, formerly a sawmill but now a private house, and follow the track as it curves right. Keep straight on past the houses on your left, noticing the track which ascends to your right towards Padley Gorge, for that is your way after visiting Padley Chapel.

PADLEY CHAPEL - was the gatehouse of Padley Manor, the foundations of which can still be seen. The top floor of the gatehouse was used as the chapel; today the congregation sits on the ground floor level and the altar is on the first floor, its original position. The manor was owned by the Eyre family and then later through marriage passed to the Fitzherberts in the 16th century. Both families were Roman Catholics. During the reign of Elizabeth Catholics were under extreme pressure, many being forced to renounce their faith, while others refused and were jailed for life or executed. The story of these times is recorded in the stained glass windows to be seen in the chapel today. In 1561 Sir Thomas Fitzherbert would not renounce his faith and was therefore jailed. He died thirty years later in the Tower. On 12th July, 1588, two Roman Catholic priests, Robert Ludlam and Nicholas Garlick were arrested at Padley. Twelve days later, along with another priest, Richard Sympson, they were hung, drawn and quartered Derby. In 1933 the chapel was acquired and restored, and made into a permanent memorial to the Padley martyrs. On opening the door the window in front of you portrays the finding of the altar stone 24th August, 1933. The chapel's hammer beam roof dates back the 14th century, two of the beams carrying carved angels bearing shields.

Retrace your steps from the chapel, and where the track dips down to Padley Mill, turn left and ascend into Padley Gorge. Or past the houses and into the wood the path levels out and you have thoroughly enjoyable walk through oaks, Scots pine and birch trees. Many species of plants can be seen both in the wood a surrounding area. There are clumps of buckler fern, wood sorrel, bog violet and lesser celandine. A variety of birds also inhabit the area and you will more than likely see several wrens and possibly a Jay.

At the top of the wood and on level ground, keep to the left-hand side of Burbage Brook and follow it to the head of the shallow valley. Near the top is a wooden bridge on your right; cross this a follow the path through further trees until you gain the stile above the entrance to Longshaw Lodge. Cross the road to Fox House and the end of your walk.

REMEMBER AND OBSERVE THE COUNTRY CODE

Enjoy the countryside and respect its life and work.

Guard against all risk of fire.

Fasten all gates.

Keep your dogs under close control.

 **Keep to public paths across farmland.**

Use gates and stiles to cross fences, hedges and walls.

Leave livestock, crops and machinery alone.

Take your litter home - pack it in; pack it out.

Help to keep all water clean.

Protect wildlife, plants and trees.

Take special care on country roads

Make no unnecessary noise.

THE HIKER'S CODE

✿ *Hike only along marked routes – do not leave the trail.*

✿ *Use stiles to climb fences; close gates.*

✿ *Camp only in designated campsites.*

✿ *Carry a light-weight stove.*

✿ *Leave the trail cleaner than you found it.*

✿ *Leave flowers and plants for others to enjoy.*

✿ *Keep dogs on a leash.*

✿ *Protect and do not disturb wildlife.*

✿ *Use the trail at your own risk.*

✿ *Leave only your thanks and footprints – take nothing but photographs.*

EQUIPMENT NOTES
.... some personal thoughts

BOOTS - *preferably with a full leather upper, of medium weight, with a vibram sole. I always add a foam cushioned insole to help cushion the base of my feet.*

SOCKS - *I generally wear two thick pairs as this helps minimise blisters. The inner pair are of loop stitch variety and approximately 80% wool. The outer are a thick rib pair of approximately 80% wool.*

WATERPROOFS - *for general walking I wear a T shirt or cotton shirt with a cotton wind jacket on top. You generate heat as you walk and I prefer to layer my clothes to avoid getting too hot. Depending on the season will dictate how many layers you wear. In soft rain I just use my wind jacket for I know it quickly dries out. In heavy or consistant rain I slip on a neoprene lined cagoule, and although hot and clammy it does keep me reasonably dry. Only in extreme conditions will I don overtrousers, much preferring to get wet and feel comfortable. I never wear gaiters!*

FOOD - *as I walk I carry bars of chocolate, for they provide instant energy and are light to carry. In winter a flask of hot coffee is welcome. I never carry water and find no hardship from not doing so, but this is a personal matter! From experience I find the more I drink the more I want and sweat. You should always carry some extra food such as Kendal Mint Cake, for emergencies.*

RUCKSACKS - *for day walking I use a climbing rucksack of about 40 litre capacity and although it leaves excess space it does mean that the sac is well padded, with an internal frame and padded shoulder straps. Inside apart from the basics for one day I carry gloves, balaclava, spare pullover and a pair of socks.*

MAP & COMPASS - *when I am walking I always have the relevant map - preferably 1:25,000 scale - open in my hand. This enables me to constantly check that I am walking the right way. In case of bad weather I carry a compass, which once mastered gives you complete confidence in thick cloud or mist.*

WALK RECORD CHART

Date Walked

CASTLETON AREA -

CASTLETON VILLAGE WALK - 4 MILES ....

CAVE DALE AND THE WINNATS - 5 MILES ....

MAM TOR - 5 MILES ....

LOSE HILL - 5 1/2 MILES.......................

HOPE AREA -

WIN HILL (SOUTHERN ROUTE) - 6 MILES.......................

WIN HILL (NORTHERN ROUTE) - 8 MILES ....

BRADWELL & SHATTON MOOR - 6 MILES ....

HATHERSAGE AREA -

HATHERSAGE VILLAGE WALK - 3 MILES ....

OFFERTON MOOR - 6,8,10 MILES ....

STANAGE EDGE - 5 1/2 MILES ....

PADLEY CHAPEL & LONGSHAW - 4 MILES ....

THE JOHN MERRILL WALK BADGE

Complete six of the walks in this book and get the above special walk badge. Badges are a black cloth with walking man embroidered in four colours and measure - 3 1/2" in diameter.

BADGE ORDER FORM

Date and details of walks completed....................................

....

NAME ....

ADDRESS ....

....

Price: £2.50 each including postage, VAT and signed completion certificate. Amount enclosed (Payable to Trail Crest Publications) ..

From: TRAIL CREST PUBLICATIONS Ltd.,
Winster, Matlock, Derbyshire. DE4 2DQ.

✆ Winster (0629) 650454 - 24hr answering service.
FAX: Winster (0629) 650416

************ **YOU MAY PHOTOCOPY THIS FORM** *********
"I'VE DONE A JOHN MERRILL WALK" T SHIRT -
Emerald Green with white lettering and walking man logo. Send £7.00 to Trail Crest Publications stating size required.

OTHER BOOKS by John N. Merrill Published by TRAIL CREST PUBLICATIONS Ltd.

CIRCULAR WALK GUIDES -

SHORT CIRCULAR WALKS IN THE PEAK DISTRICT
CIRCULAR WALKS IN WESTERN PEAKLAND
SHORT CIRCULAR WALKS IN THE STAFFORDSHIRE MOORLANDS
SHORT CIRCULAR WALKS - TOWNS & VILLAGES OF THE PEAK DISTRICT
SHORT CIRCULAR WALKS AROUND MATLOCK
SHORT CIRCULAR WALKS IN THE DUKERIES
SHORT CIRCULAR WALKS IN SOUTH YORKSHIRE
SHORT CIRCULAR WALKS IN SOUTH DERBYSHIRE
SHORT CIRCULAR WALKS AROUND BUXTON
SHORT CIRCULAR WALKS IN THE HOPE VALLEY
40 SHORT CIRCULAR WALKS IN THE PEAK DISTRICT
CIRCULAR WALKS ON KINDER & BLEAKLOW
SHORT CIRCULAR WALKS IN SOUTH NOTTINGHAMSHIRE
SHIRT CIRCULAR WALKS IN CHESHIRE
SHORT CIRCULAR WALKS IN WEST YORKSHIRE
CIRCULAR WALKS TO PEAK DISTRICT AIRCRAFT WRECKS by John Mason
CIRCULAR WALKS IN THE DERBYSHIRE DALES
SHORT CIRCULAR WALKS IN EAST DEVON
SHORT CIRCULAR WALKS AROUND HARROGATE
SHORT CIRCULAR WALKS IN CHARNWOOD FOREST
LONG CIRCULAR WALKS IN THE PEAK DISTRICT
LONG CIRCULAR WALKS IN THE STAFFORDSHIRE MOORLANDS

CANAL WALKS -

VOL 1 - DERBYSHIRE & NOTTINGHAMSHIRE
VOL 2 - CHESHIRE & STAFFORDSHIRE
VOL 3 - STAFFORDSHIRE
VOL 4 - THE CHESHIRE RING
VOL 5 - LINCOLNSHIRE & NOTTINGHAMSHIRE
VOL 6 - SOUTH YORKSHIRE
VOL 7 - THE TRENT & MERSEY CANAL

JOHN MERRILL DAY CHALLENGE WALKS -

WHITE PEAK CHALLENGE WALK
DARK PEAK CHALLENGE WALK
PEAK DISTRICT END TO END WALKS
STAFFORDSHIRE MOORLANDS CHALLENGE WALK
THE LITTLE JOHN CHALLENGE WALK
YORKSHIRE DALES CHALLENGE WALK
NORTH YORKSHIRE MOORS CHALLENGE WALK
LAKELAND CHALLENGE WALK
THE RUTLAND WATER CHALLENGE WALK
MALVERN HILLS CHALLENGE WALK
THE SALTER'S WAY
THE SNOWDON CHALLENGE

INSTRUCTION & RECORD -
HIKE TO BE FIT......STROLLING WITH JOHN
THE JOHN MERRILL WALK RECORD BOOK

MULTIPLE DAY WALKS -
THE RIVERS'S WAY
PEAK DISTRICT: HIGH LEVEL ROUTE
PEAK DISTRICT MARATHONS
THE LIMEY WAY
THE PEAKLAND WAY

COAST WALKS & NATIONAL TRAILS -
ISLE OF WIGHT COAST PATH
PEMBROKESHIRE COAST PATH
THE CLEVELAND WAY

PEAK DISTRICT HISTORICAL GUIDES -
A to Z GUIDE OF THE PEAK DISTRICT
DERBYSHIRE INNS - an A to Z guide
HALLS AND CASTLES OF THE PEAK DISTRICT & DERBYSHIRE
TOURING THE PEAK DISTRICT & DERBYSHIRE BY CAR
DERBYSHIRE FOLKLORE
PUNISHMENT IN DERBYSHIRE
CUSTOMS OF THE PEAK DISTRICT & DERBYSHIRE
WINSTER - a souvenir guide
ARKWRIGHT OF CROMFORD
LEGENDS OF DERBYSHIRE
TALES FROM THE MINES by Geoffrey Carr
PEAK DISTRICT PLACE NAMES by Martin Spray

JOHN MERRILL'S MAJOR WALKS -
TURN RIGHT AT LAND'S END
WITH MUSTARD ON MY BACK
TURN RIGHT AT DEATH VALLEY
EMERALD COAST WALK

COLOUR GUIDES -
THE PEAK DISTRICT..........Something to remember her by.

SKETCH BOOKS -
NORTH STAFFORDSHIRE SKETCHBOOK by John Creber
SKETCHES OF THE PEAK DISTRICT

IN PREPARATION -
SHORT CIRCULAR WALKS IN THE YORKSHIRE DALES
SHORT CIRCULAR WALKS IN THE LAKE DISTRICT
SHORT CIRCULAR WALKS IN NORTH YORKSHIRE MOORS
CHARNWOOD FOREST CHALLENGE WALK
FOOTPATHS OF THE WORLD - Vol I - NORTH AMERICA
HIKING IN NEW MEXICO - 7 VOLUMES
Vol I - The Sandia and Manzano Mountains.

☞ **Full list from TRAIL CREST PUBLICATIONS Ltd.,**
Winster, Matlock, Derbyshire. DE4 2DQ